CULTURE IS LIFE

Aboriginal and Torres Strait Islander readers are advised that this book may contain images and names of people who have died.

CULTURE
IS LIFE

WAYNE QUILLIAM

A photographic
exploration of Aboriginal
and Torres Strait Islander
peoples in modern Australia

Hardie Grant

BOOKS

Foreword

RHODA ROBERTS AO
As we move into the twenty-first century, I am so inspired by the
work of our artists and the new mediums we are using to share
our culture. Photography brings a new strength for showing
the depth and diversity of who we are and why country is so
important. Through the lens of Wayne Quilliam's images, the
tangible and the intangible is captured; there is the trust of those
being photographed and the truth is encapsulated. It is like the
mapping of country, and he has created a new archive of truth-
telling. The photo never lies: from the joy of our young men and
women dancing, to the beauty, diversity and what may appear as
the harshness of country, Wayne's images are like a new gaze that
reads country, with the portraits telling of the trauma and hinting
at the glint of strength for our future. As we regard his images,
a thousand stories of tens of thousands of years are observed
and told, from the old to the young, with the spirituality and the
self-empowerment that is bubbling and growing, and we get a
glimpse of our future warriors and tradition bearers. Thank you,
Wayne – we often hate getting our photos taken – it's like a trip
to the dentist, but the smiles through the eyes that you have
captured bring pride, in the old ways of our people, standing tall,
and the empowerment of who we are. There is no need for talk,
the images speak for themselves and this book will be another
legacy for the wisdom seekers of tomorrow.

'When telling me stories of country, my father would remind me of
our inherited birthright and the legacy and the obligation required
if I was to identify as a Widjabul woman.

Like it was for his father and his father's fathers before him, and
the long line of our grandmothers, this was kinship and we had
to hold tight to what the Bundjalung had fought for. As I grew and
travelled the world, he would remind me in his letters and our
talks: "You never forget, some things are in safekeeping, but now
is the time to speak up – there is a purpose and you, my sister,
are in service to your peoples."

I actually thought when I was young that we came from royalty.
"You are one of the lucky ones," he would whisper. "We have
everything, you know the system, have an education and,

with your mixed blood, you have a pulse in both worlds, but you will always be learning and every day there will be lessons. Look beyond the horizon of your being, its bigger than all of us, and learn to listen well."

I'm still working on that one – but I was given the essential tools to know my belonging. Like many, there have been those heartfelt moments where I questioned my worth. But now, entering my sixty-second year, family, kinship and culture come first.

When our people talk of the past, about the knowing that will give us the guiding steps for the future, they could not have been more right: knowing country, and how to manage the seasons, will ensure a planet for the coming children. Culture is our advantage – it's complex, and sadly we are now facing a crisis like never before and we must ensure the continuous reclamation of the stories, the languages, the revitalisations of songline and the dance, and the honouring of our cultural protocols and wisdom. This is what makes us whole, the stories are the knowledge that tell us of our land, sea and sky. I am so fortunate to have a job that can ensure the visibility of, and give voice to, who we are. Culture is everything.'

Culture is ...

'We have social rules and structures, our lifestyles are well organised by our gurruṯu [kinship] system. We stand firm, stand strong, learn the sacred designs of our paintings, the songs, the dances, the stories, the contours of my lands, to keep them safe in our hearts.

We have to learn from the land and how it defines our spiritual affiliations to it; it helps to understand whose land it is. It is sovereign and ancient, this web of civilisation of the Yolŋu kinship structure, it is everlasting and embedded in the ancestral clans of north-east Arnhem Land and the new contemporary clans today that still continue to light the fires in our ancient lands.

Our intellect is sacred miny'tji [clan designs]; our homelands and ancestral hearth of ancient origin, knowledge and law flows from these clans, we are the people founded in these ancient lands and body of waters.

We cannot fully explain the concept, because we not only understand it, we also feel, touch, smell, taste and hear it. Thus speaks the songlines/knowledge and law in the languages that we spoke then and speak today.'
Merrkiyawuy Ganambarr

'Culture is as simple as being part of my family and as complex as walking on country and feeling dwarfed by everything around me – the land, the deep history, the memories and the sense that I am standing in the places my ancestors shaped and cared for.'
Wesley Enoch AM

'For First Nations Australians the visual and performing arts are the most powerful way by which we may know the world and give meaning to everything in it. For more than two thousand generations we have passed on all knowledge of geography, the sciences, medicine and humanity through the visual and performing arts. For the Indigenous people of this land the arts have never been a luxury, rather a necessity. Our culture is our knowledge, our knowledge our survival and, above all, it provides us with the belonging we need to exist.'
Deborah Cheetham AO

The journey

The memories, the experiences, the friendships created through my 'calling' as a dreamer, storyteller, artist and documenter of history is undefinable.

The adventure began as a sixteen-year-old in the Royal Australian Navy. My stomach churned with excitement as my legs dangled out of a British Army helicopter lifting off the grey steel deck of the aircraft carrier docked in Hong Kong harbour. We were travelling with the elite SAS group to the border outpost dividing China and the New Territories to patrol the twenty-foot barbed wire fence. I asked one of the soldiers about the material entangled along the perimeter: it was from strips of clothing of those who did not survive the climb. Excitement turned to reality as I realised my time as a naive Tasmanian boy had evaporated.

Returning to civilian life as a barman, bouncer, chimney sweep, shooter, tiler, and every job in between, fed a yearning to learn about culture, with the camera becoming a unique tool to engage and interact with community.

It is difficult to truly encapsulate the love and gratitude I have for my parents, Meg and Bob, who give so much and ask for so little. They continue to inspire, and every accolade, every achievement is for and because of them. Incredible artist and brother Mick connects me back to country as little sister Nicolle connects me to family. My three children, Nathan, Aaron and Tanisha, along with my ever-entertaining grandkids, Tylah, Keelie, Lilliarna and Maddyson, make life special. Born a creative spirit forever destined to travel, the experiment of normality didn't work for me. That was until one fateful night I met this incredible person who not only understood the complexities of wanderlust but actively participated. My incredible wife, Jodie, is my inspiration.

My career, my life is evolutionary: every day I create, explore and challenge myself as an artist and storyteller. Of necessity, transforming my vision through other mediums including film and digital art inspires me to new heights – my career has just begun. A sincere message to everyone that we couldn't include in this book: the best is yet to come, and for those names we missed, sincerest apologies, every effort was made.
Adjunct Professor Wayne Quilliam

Beguiled, lured, enticed
by the tides of change,
we stand in the shallows
gasping for air.

A Pitjantjatjara/Nyungar man from Western Australia, Trevor Jamieson is without doubt one of Australia's finest actors. His roles as Fingerbone Bill in the remake of the film *Storm Boy* and playing artist Albert Namatjira on stage are iconic.

Australia's first Aboriginal community Surf Life Saving club, Walngawu Djakamirri – meaning 'carer of life' in Yolŋu Matha, the language of north-east Arnhem Land – was established in 2009. The club operates most of the year except during the wet season, due to baru (crocodiles) and the deadly box jellyfish.

Ex-policewoman Jarin Baigent comes from an impressive lineage of inspiring Aboriginal women who have been pioneers of positive change. Her grandmother, Millie Ingram, is a longstanding advocate for Aboriginal rights, and her great-grandmother was involved in the Day of Mourning in 1938.

'I've always been passionate about my culture. I was raised to respect and be proud of my culture and who I am. It's always been something I've felt responsible for upholding. In everything I've ever done I've tried to encourage and to educate those around me who might not know enough – if they're willing to learn. Learning about our culture is a valuable gift.'

Black represents the skin and spirit of people, yellow is for the sun, the giver of life, and the red signifies our connection to land.

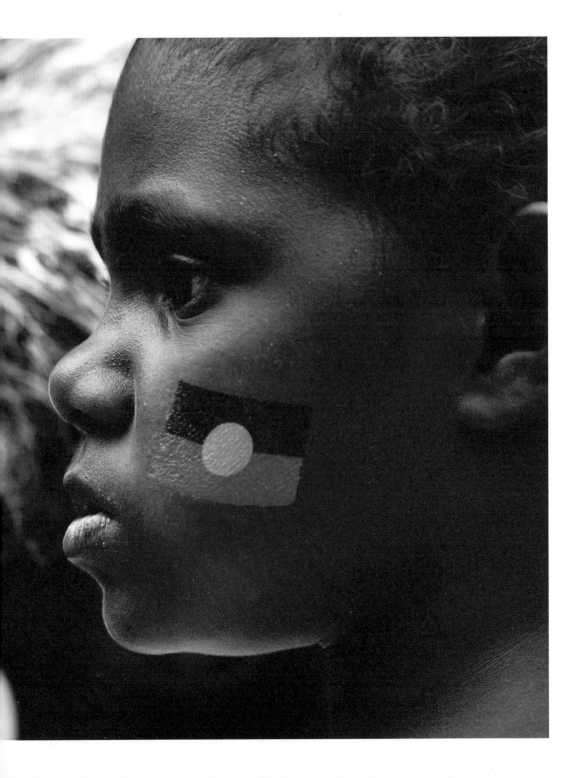

In 2005, the inaugural Dreamtime at the G Australian Rules Football match was played on the Melbourne Cricket Ground. The match is played each year during National Reconciliation Week, which is a significant week for the Indigenous community.

Right
Tanya Hosch is the general manager of inclusion and social policy at the AFL and a passionate advocate for change. A proud Torres Strait Islander social activist, her work has catalysed monumental shifts towards equal opportunity for Indigenous people.

Centre
Dusty Martin, wearing
an Aboriginal-designed
guernsey for Dreamtime
at the G, leads the
Richmond Tigers onto
the field.

Below
'Love that photo.
Walking out, I was
feeling very proud to
be representing my
culture and my family.
I had all my mob in the
grandstands watching,
and to have my two
sons walk out with
my team was one of
the highlights of my
footy career – my
culture is everything
that I believe in and
represent. My culture
is the foundation of
my life.'
Nathan Lovett-Murray

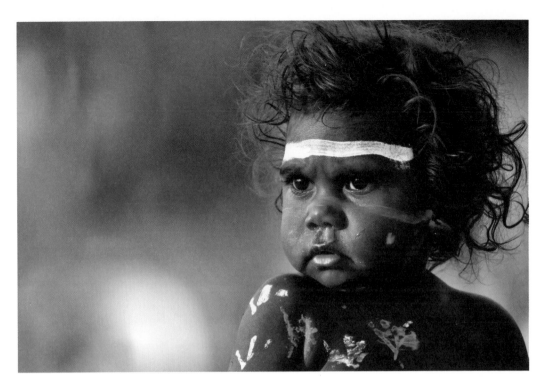

Above

This photo means so much to me, as an old friend, Uncle Frank from Elcho Island, said to me after I took it, 'Wayne, I want you to come every year to photograph family and community. The photos will keep our spirit alive for the young ones.'

He left us not long after – his words remind me of the important work to be done.

Opposite

The Yolŋu people in north-east Arnhem Land are divided into two different moieties, Yirritja and Dhuwa. The little ones belong to the same moiety as their father, and their mother belongs to the other moiety.

'What culture meant to our people before colonialism has almost been completely destroyed.

The Earth is our mother – we are the land, and the land is us. We knew our place in the ecological scheme of things as the caretakers, custodians and guardians of a sacred duty and the law of the land. The unchecked criminal genocide and resultant ecocide over the last 250 years has seen a deliberate attempt to erase that. Without our land we are nothing.

Our strict laws, governing our people and our relationships, are the basis of our culture. For the Holocaust survivors, colonised refugees, and fringe and ghetto dwellers today, our culture means fighting for our survival, resisting the invading forces, the assimilation, demanding sovereign recognition, restitution, repatriation, a truth commission and/or an internationally scrutinised war crimes trial – for justice, healing and harmony.

Peace on Earth in our time. If you don't fight, you lose – that's our culture today.'
Robbie Thorpe

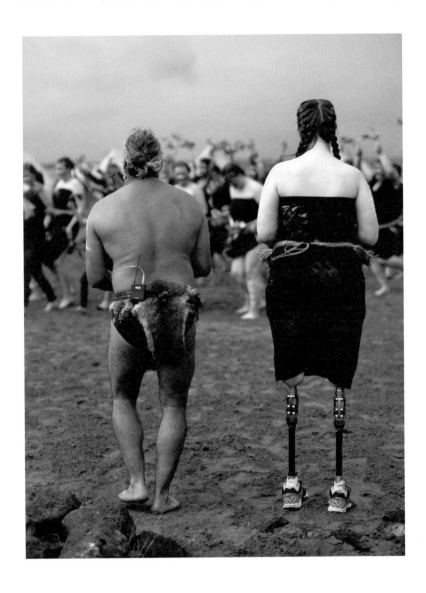

These two images encompass cultural modernity: one an ethnographic portrait reflecting the strength of the past while the other recontextualises how we live in modern society.

Covering more than 100,000 square kilometres of South Australia and home to around 3000 people, the APY (Aṉangu Pitjantjatjara Yankunytjatjara) Lands are one of the most incredible places on Earth. Commissioned to document the journey of the *Kungkarangkalpa: Seven Sisters Songline*, I had journeyed with old friend and artistic director of the project Wesley Enoch into the desert to experience a series of unpredictable moments. Watching Wesley sit on top of a Troopy (4WD Landcruiser) absorbing the essence of inma (ceremony) in the cold darkness of the desert evoked powerful memories.

What was even more interesting was experiencing one culture in two events. As I was sitting having a cup of tea after days of recording inma, the old ladies said to me, 'Wayne, no more dancing today, we have another ceremony, important ceremony.' The laughing had me suspicious, as I had been caught out many times before by tricksters.

As we all drove into town, I was thinking about supplies but headed across to the red, sandy oval surrounded by 'bush' cars brightly painted in the colours of the AFL Bulldogs and Eagles. It was the Footy Grand Final. Seeing the mob painted up for traditional ceremony one day and then wearing crazy wigs and giant hands cheering on family is indelibly burnt into my consciousness.

In 1967, history was made when Australia voted overwhelmingly to amend the constitution, ensuring Aboriginal and Torres Strait Islander peoples had the same rights as other Australians.

Fifty years later, a large group of people who had worked tirelessly on the campaign were brought together in Sydney to board a flight to Canberra famously known as the 1967 Referendum Flight. The Qantas plane, adorned with Balarinji designs and an Indigenous crew on board, arrived in the nation's capital to a sea of wellwishers forming a guard of honour on the tarmac.

SORRY
DAY

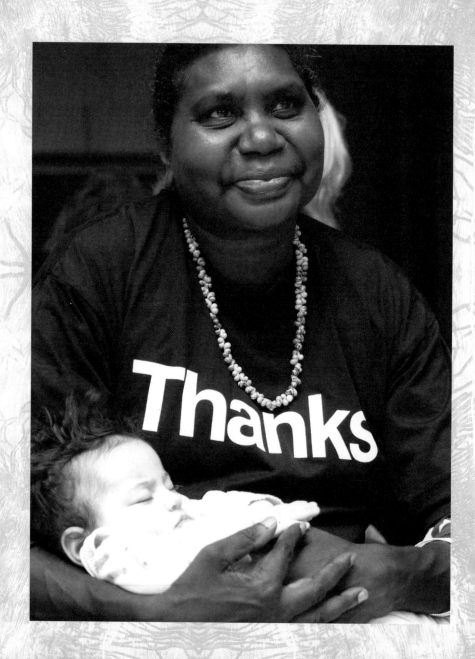

The Apology was an event like no other, an evolving landscape of emotional spot fires destined to change lives forever. Days before that nation-defining moment, we gathered at the Tent Embassy to march on Parliament House protesting the Intervention. We had the attention of the nation, and a platform for articulating past and present injustices as raw, unbridled emotion unified the people that had travelled to the nation's capital to hear that word 'Sorry'.

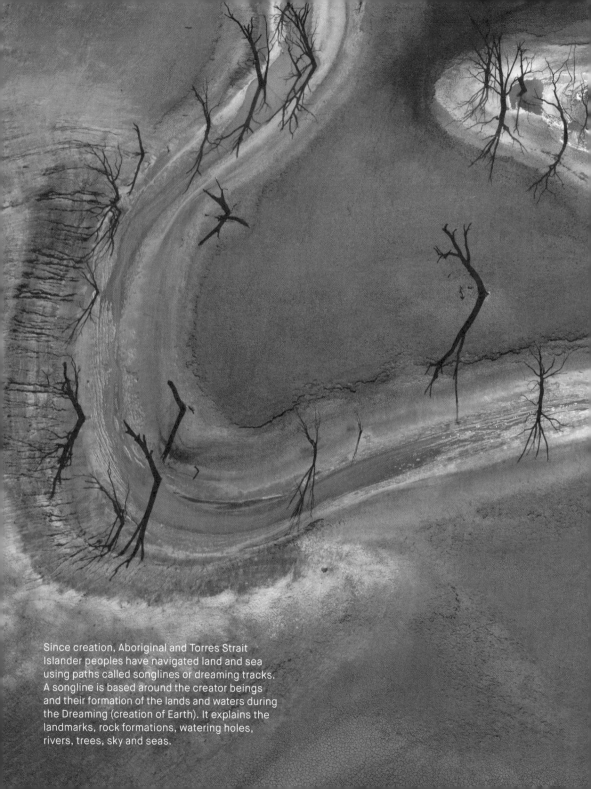

Since creation, Aboriginal and Torres Strait Islander peoples have navigated land and sea using paths called songlines or dreaming tracks. A songline is based around the creator beings and their formation of the lands and waters during the Dreaming (creation of Earth). It explains the landmarks, rock formations, watering holes, rivers, trees, sky and seas.

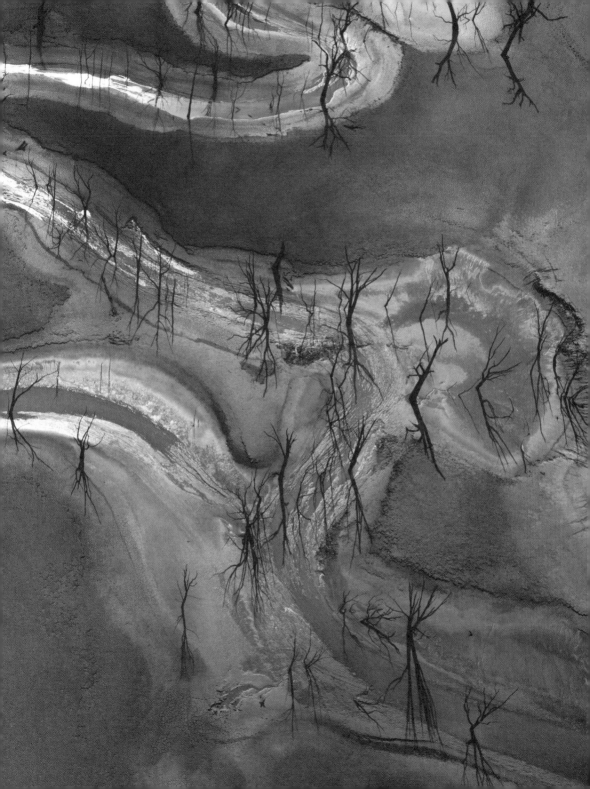

Above
Aden Ridgeway, Jackie Huggins,
Shelly Reys, Linda Burney,
Pat Dodson and Karen Mundine

'Culture is a complex carpet. Each
strand represents language, land,
sea, creation, food, purpose,
spirituality, family (living and past).
They weave in, around and through
one another, creating the very fabric
that holds communities together.'
Shelly Reys

Right
Activist, film producer, health
worker and tireless advocate for
the rights of Indigenous people and
Bunuba woman, Dr June Oscar is the
Aboriginal and Torres Strait Islander
Social Justice Commissioner. The
accolades and plaudits Professor
Tom Calma has received in the many
roles he has filled are a testament to
the incredible work he has done for
our communities.

Above
Deborah Cheetham

Above left
Rhoda Roberts

Below
'Culture is the interconnectedness of past and future, our ancestral link to the memory and way of life that came before us. It is our touchstone to hold, love and grow before we too face our own ascension, taking our place among the ancestors. Culture is the gift to our descendants as it was gifted to us, our rite of passage and a space for each of us to lay our piece down in life's continuum. Culture is my story, their story, your story, our story. Culture is us.'
Sam Cook

Centre
Michael O'Loughlin, Jeff McMullen and David Liddiard

Below
'Our ancestors' past, Our children's future, Our culture, Your culture.

We are connected to our ancestors by speaking and singing our language.

Dhagungwurrung dhum-djerring – Our language speaking.

Dhagungwurrung yenga-k – Our language singing.

We should leave this world a better place for our children.

Build their future with them. Include their ideas and dreams.

Bunbunarik wurrdhadindu ngarrnga-k-gu – Children's ideas.

Bunbunarik wurrdhadindu yarragin-un – Children's dreams.

Our culture is endemic to our country. Our stories are our ancestors weaving. Our symbols are a continual echo. Our mind and soul is our country.

Durn durn biik nugal-nganjin – Mind country ours.

Murrup biik nugal-nganjin – Soul country ours.

You have an opportunity to connect with this country and understand where you live.

The depth of your understanding is a journey, making new tracks together.

Ngarrnga-k-gu gungi wagabil – Understand deep.

Yuwang-ngal-in barring wurrdhadindu munganin – Together tracks many make.'
Mick Harding

In many urban communities throughout Australia, young boys are taken back out on country to learn the old ways. This mob from Mount Isa are taught bush skills as the old people share stories of the ancestors.

'Sis, can you hear that? Sounds like munchkins.'

Suddenly at the top of the rise, a sea of screaming barefooted kids burst out of the bush and began running towards Cathy. Smiling and laughing, Cathy hid behind me as I transformed from photographer into a human shield while we became swamped by overly enthusiastic kids.

Travelling with Cathy Freeman and her foundation to document community has been a passion for many years. The incredible memories and moments make me smile daily. After working at the local school on Galiwin'ku, a small island in the Arafura Sea, some of the women asked Cathy to go for a run at the back of the island, several kilometres from the community, and we were waiting for them to arrive.

Fathers, sons, brothers and
nephews from across the
country gathered en masse in
Melbourne to take part in the
Warriors Walk. Coming together
to challenge the mainstream
media's vilification of Indigenous
men as domestic abusers,
we peacefully articulated our
solidarity with all women.

Welcoming

Indigenous media plays an extremely important role in the maintenance and strengthening of culture. We have a national newspaper, the *Koori Mail*, television channel NITV, more than a hundred Remote Indigenous Broadcasting Services (RIBS), and twenty-eight urban and regional radio services that are essential to the sharing of information throughout our communities.

Each year, First Nations Media organises a conference on country, bringing us together to develop new skills and share stories. Nearly 900 kilometres out of Darwin, the remote community of Lajamanu invited a large contingent of Indigenous media practitioners from across Australia onto their traditional homelands, and this photo represents the strength and knowledge of the Warlpiri people who welcomed us.

FASHION

A new generation of Indigenous fashion designers is changing the narrative when it comes to incorporating art and culture. Rural, remote and urban creatives continue to push the boundaries by incorporating traditional and contemporary culture in denim and t-shirts, jewellery and swimwear in bold, vivid colours, appearing in magazines and on catwalks across the globe.

Above
Hans Ahwang

Opposite
'My name is Rikki Jane McAdam and I am Larrakia, Kungarakan, Arrernte and Kija from both sets of my grandparents. Culture to me is everything, without it we are nothing.'

Ochre plays an important role in ceremony and art, and is the most recognised natural material used by Traditional Owners. This colourful soft stone comes in a range of browns, reds, sandy yellows, whites, greys, moody purples and even greens. It is infused with various natural gum resins or with oils and fats derived from animals (creatures such as emus and kangaroos) to bind, retain its colour and preserve.

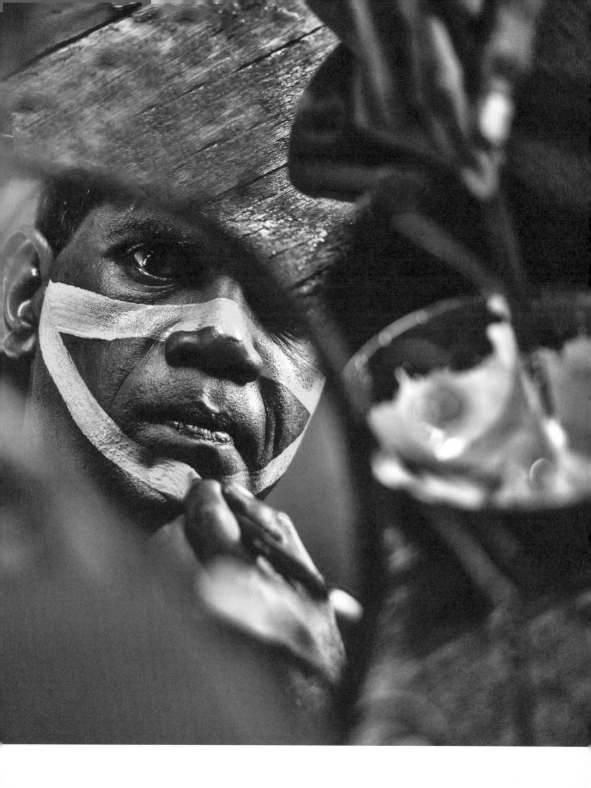

NAIDOC WEEK

(National Aborigines and Islanders Day of Observance Committee)

On Australia Day 1938, a march was organised through the streets of Sydney protesting the status and treatment of Aboriginal and Torres Strait Islander peoples. Recognised as one of the first major civil rights gatherings in the world, it became known as the Day of Mourning and for many years was known as Aborigines Day. In 1955, it was decided that Aborigines Day should include a celebration of Aboriginal culture, heritage and achievement. This is now celebrated as NAIDOC Week, which highlights the achievements of Indigenous people all over Australia.

Centre
Jill Gallagher, Michael Graham, Ken Wyatt and Rod Jackson

Below
Andrew Pitt, Terri Janke, John Paul Janke and Anita Heiss

Opposite
'Our cultural life begins generations before we are born, and continues after we die for many more generations – this is the genetic memory of our ancestors that lives in our murrup [spirit].'
Mandy Nicholson

Funeral, burial and cleansing ceremonies not only play an especially important role in Indigenous culture, they differ greatly throughout the country. These rituals involve the whole community and may take many days, or several years. From region to region, the use of body paint, ceremonial headdress, and the designs on spears and shields are integral to the connection of the living and the dead.

THREE
RIVERS

Opposite
'I am a young, proud Aboriginal girl. I have travelled the world, explored new places and talked at the United Nations. But what I love the most is going to our gatherings, getting painted up, dancing and learning culture from my Aunties and Uncles.'
Tanisha Quilliam

Millewa or Tongala are the traditional names of the Murray River. From a small trickle near Mount Kosciuszko that grows into an important songline for Aboriginal people living along its banks and floodplains, the river divests into the Dungala, Yakoa and Gaiyila, which meet near the border towns of Echuca and Moama. Recognised as a significant gathering site, this area is the location for Aboriginal people to gather and celebrate culture at the Three Rivers Festival.

Uncle Jimmy Little was far more than a country music star; he was a true gentleman of unequalled spirit. A Yorta Yorta man from Cummerangunja Mission, he became a household name with his song 'Royal Telephone', then went on to acting and performing in many different genres. I had photographed him many times over the years, but this one was special. I was about to approach him as he sat in the shadows of Parliament House in Canberra getting ready to perform, a reflective moment of solitude. As I began to turn on my heels so as not to interrupt, he raised his head, nodded and smiled. This was our last photo.

Like most Indigenous children, the kids of Bawaka, a small community south of Yirrkala in Arnhem Land, learn to fish, gather and hunt from an early age. Traditional learning is a natural and progressive system that encompasses things like knowing the seven seasons or what is moiety – Yirratja, and kinship – Dhuwa.

Photographer Jimmy Nelson
from Amsterdam reached out to
me to collaborate on a series of
images that would feature in his
new book *Homage to Humanity*.
After consulting with the
communities of Mowanjum and
Lombadina in Western Australia,
we agreed to meet in Broome.
As usual, it was the kids who
provided the entertainment
as we searched for the right
location, some jumping off the
red cliffs onto the pure white
sands of Cape Leveque. Jimmy
experienced Aussie Rules
Football for the first time as the
kids kicked the footy around the
wetlands outside Mowanjum.

Two lands, one vision.

Connection.

Kids of Galiwin'ku, off the Northern Territory coast, play in torrential rain. This photo was taken just after Cyclone Lam hit in February 2015 and prior to a less severe Cyclone Nathan that followed a month later.

Seeking clarity, becoming one,
we are the land, the air, the
water, the bush, and every living
thing in it.

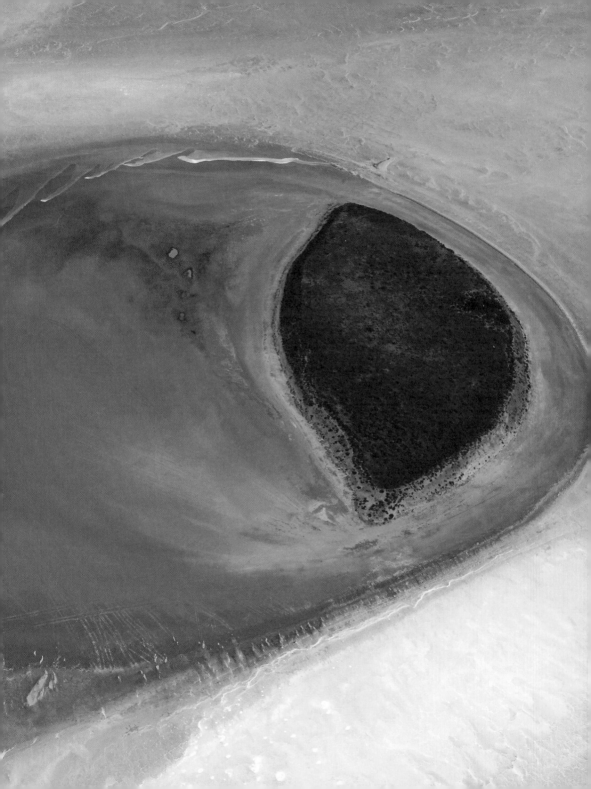

Above

'At the heart of it – at the very guts of what I do – it's about the jarjum [children] – the young ones. It's about them living in a world worth living in. It's about them being strong in culture and identity – knowing the strength of our history. It's about our true strength and knowing that they are connected – to each other – and to our old ones. If they know the histories and understand the strength of the old ones, what they lived through and what they suffered, then maybe they will see that same strength in themselves – the strength of the old ones – and celebrate the truth and the remarkable beauty of a culture that is theirs.'

Marcus Hughes

Below

Michael McLeod is a Ngarrindjeri Monaro man from Southern New South Wales. At two years old, he was stolen from his parents and made a ward of the state. By ten, he was using drugs and alcohol and in his twenties he was living on the streets of Sydney. Today he is CEO of a multimillion dollar tech company, an acclaimed artist and one of the most supportive and giving people we have in our community.

Above
True leaders share their visions and inspire others to explore the possibilities. I couldn't think of two more inspirational leaders than Kirstie Parker and Dot West.

Below
Karla Grant is far more than a producer, director, reporter and presenter, she is a voice of reason, a voice of our people.

Above

'Culture ... is reflected in the hundreds of things I do and the decisions I make every day. It's not conscious thought – it's in my DNA. My Aboriginal culture is strong in sharing – sharing possessions, celebrating good times together, sharing the bad times and staying strong for each other. My family and I live our culture's values and I see myself as a reflection of my Aboriginal heritage.'
David Liddiard

Below

From Indulkana in South Australia, Pitjantjatjara woman Lowitja O'Donoghue and her two sisters were taken from their parents and sent to Colebrook Children's Home. Prohibited at the home from speaking language or practising her culture, against all odds Lowitja became the first Aboriginal woman to be inducted into the new Order of Australia, becoming Australian of the Year and receiving numerous international accolades for her work as an advocate for Aboriginal rights. I remember photographing her for the first time in the early nineties when she was appointed chairperson of ATSIC. Her cheeky smile and disarming humour masked the essence of strength and fortitude hidden beneath.

Above
Samantha Harris walks the runway in the shadow of Uluṟu as she inspires Indigenous people across the globe. One of Australia's most successful models, she started her career at the age of thirteen and featured on the cover of *Vogue Australia* at eighteen.

Samantha is passionate about stamping out racism and empowering Indigenous Australians, about showing the beauty of Indigenous women. Photographing her wearing Indigenous designs gives you a sense of pride. Black pride translates into the way young men and women in community look at her and are inspired by her.

Below
'Culture has been my biggest healer.

As someone who has struggled quite openly in my battles with mental illness, on reflection, the biggest thing that has helped me manage my illness has been culture.

It brings me safety and contentment in a world that speeds along at a million miles an hour.

Culture teaches me valuable lessons, lessons taught by the old people (the ancestors) through stories. These stories kept us safe and protected. By living through the very values of our old stories, I have learnt to get closer to the values of love, care, respect, humility, compassion – values deeply embedded within the stories that make up our culture.'
Joe Williams

Sitting atop the Dhupuma Plateau in Arnhem Land, Yolŋu families prepare to share bunggul (dance) and manikay (song) at the internationally recognised Garma Festival. When I began documenting the festival in its early days, I remember sitting next to Mandawuy Yunupingu and him saying, 'Wayne, listen to manikay, feel wangarr, you will understand'. Every time I sit on the ground capturing the essence of any ceremony, I hear his voice and his spirit.

Intergenerational learning
is the cornerstone for the
continuance of culture.
Transference of knowledge
ensures connection to
country remains strong.

Bidyadanga hoops
Bidyadanga, from
bidyada, meaning
'emu watering hole',
is on the traditional
land of the Karajarri
people, located south
of Broome in Western
Australia. Many years
ago, the Nyangumarta,
Mangala, Juwaliny
and Yulpartja people
moved in from the
desert to form the
largest remote
Aboriginal community
in Western Australia.
Every afternoon after
school, the kids go
hunting, fishing or
shooting hoops on
the basketball court.

ALL
STARS

In 2010, fans of Rugby League converged on the Gold Coast to watch the inaugural Indigenous All Stars challenge against the NRL All Stars. The brainchild of Preston Campbell, who kicked things off as captain, the game was won by the Indigenous All Stars 16–12.

Above

Emu features prominently in many of our creation stories, like why Emu has short wings.

When Emu had very long wings, she flew from her home in the sky to join Brolga dancing by a lagoon. 'You can't dance with such long wings,' said Brolga. 'Let me clip them for you.' After cutting Emu's wings very short, cunning old Brolga spread her own long wings, which she had hidden by folding them along her back, and flew away. Now unable to fly, Emu never returned to her home in the sky.

Opposite

John Kundereri Moriarty was the first Aboriginal player selected to play football (soccer) for Australia and is co-founder of the Moriarty Foundation and Balarinji Indigenous Strategy and Design. He created the John Moriarty Football (JMF) program, which encourages Indigenous kids to use soccer for positive change, improving school attendance and achieving resilient, healthier outcomes. The programs run in Borroloola, in the remote Gulf of Carpentaria, NT; Dubbo, NSW; Kuranda, Queensland; and Tennant Creek, NT.

Above
Generally Tiwi people
don't consider
themselves to be
Aboriginal. Separated
by eighty kilometres
of crocodile-infested
ocean from mainland
Australia, they proudly
refer to themselves
as Tiwi.

Opposite
Felicia Foxx at Yabun
Festival in Sydney.

FIRST PEOPLES' ASSEMBLY

The First Peoples' Assembly of Victoria was created in 2019 to be the voice of Aboriginal people and communities for a much-anticipated Treaty.

Right
Eleanor Bourke and Jill Gallagher

Above
Jamie Lowe, Rueben Burg, Ngarra Murray, Trent Nelson, Geraldine Atkinson, Marcus Stewart, Troy McDonald, Tracey Evans and Melissa Jones

Aboriginal people living close to waterways built canoes and rafts to cross rivers, estuaries, billabongs and lakes, and to travel along ocean coastlines. Canoes were generally made from a single sheet of bark stripped from a tree, leaving what is known as a 'canoe' tree. The bark was laid over a smouldering fire to make it more pliable, then folded and tied at both ends with fibre. Rafts were simple in construction but very effective on flat water; large panels of paperbark laid on top of each other could support two or three adults and be used for fishing and waterskiing.

Ghostly figures dance to the haunting sounds of the yidaki (the Yolŋu name for the didgeridoo) — emu feathers flow as painted bodies float atop the sandy landscape. Embracing the movements, feeling the moment allows me to paint mystical compositions in tranquil shadows. This photo represents an artwork within an artwork, stories within stories, this is culture in its purest form.

Uncle Jack Charles

Megan Wilding and
Elaine Crombie in a
classic comedy sketch.

From the lush green wetlands
of the north to the burning red
sands of the centre, our children
continue to evolve our stories ...

The kids of Yuendumu play in their backyard, which happens to be the edge of the Tanami Desert at one of the largest Aboriginal communities in Central Australia. Most speak Warlpiri. They love going hunting but also swimming in the local pool. The kids are related to some of Australia's most celebrated creatives, at Warlukurlangu Artists, one of the longest-running Aboriginal-owned art centres in Central Australia. Warlukurlangu means 'belonging to fire', and is named after a Fire Dreaming site, west of the community.

FESTIVAL OF PACIFIC ARTS

Every four years, more than 2000 Indigenous artists gather at the Festival of Pacific Arts to share culture at one of the longest-running celebrations of Indigenous excellence in the world. My role as a cultural ambassador and documenter for the Australian contingent in the Solomon Islands and then Guam was a life-changing experience. Arriving at the opening ceremony around 4 am, we joined our brothers and sisters from twenty-six Pacific Nations on a beach outside of Honiara. I remember sitting close to the stage with my legs over what I thought was a furry log. When it began to move and started to squeal, I realised it was one of the pigs being gifted to each nation.

A spectacular sunrise silhouetted the graceful vakas (boats) as they arrived following their circumnavigation of the Pacific and were joined by traditional canoes from across the Solomons. For the next two weeks we shared food, dance, music, art, carving, tattooing, filmmaking, healing and ceremonial arts, fashion and design.

The community phone is unique – an essential part of many remote communities. The phone will ring and whoever is closest will answer, then the fun begins as the search commences for the person the caller is after.

When old is new.

Right

It is impossible to describe the moment when being named NAIDOC Artist of the Year. The first thing I thought of was my gratitude to and acknowledgement of every single person who walked with and guided me on this incredible journey.

Below

Jess Mauboy, William Barton and I were to be part of G'Day USA in Los Angeles, New York and Chicago as the featured artists. Walking the red carpet with people like Hugh Jackman, Nicole Kidman and Paul Hogan was a unique experience, especially when I was presented to the photography pack and one of them shouted, 'Who is he?' As I replied, 'I'm Australia's answer to Bruce Willis', the flashes became blinding, and I walked off laughing.

Above

We were in New York preparing to open the Mali Dharngurr exhibition, a series of forty-four portraits and online stories featuring Indigenous women's voices, commissioned by the United Nations and the Australian Government. After installing the work, we were discussing the running order when Tanisha said, 'Daddy, I am an Aboriginal girl, I should be speaking as well'. The diplomatic faces went from amused to perplexed when I agreed she would be joining me on the dais. A few days later we stood in front of diplomats and dignitaries from across the world and, true to her word, our little eight-year-old did the women proud.

Left

Bringing the 'Sorry, More than a Word' exhibition from Parliament House in Canberra to the home of Dr Marika was a profoundly life-changing experience. I'll always remember the morning I walked past the photos and one of the volunteers came up to me and, with a worried look on their face, said, 'People are wiping sweat all over the photo, how should we clean it?'.

In Yolŋu culture this practice relates to spiritual connection, and the photograph has never been cleaned.

Below

Jason Glanville is a Wiradjuri man who, through his selfless work, has shaped the future for many Indigenous people. Recognised as an influential leader, role model and instigator of change, he continues to inspire me to discover the meaning of self through the journey of friendship.

Above

With Estanislao (Stani) Allende Galluccio and Tom Wheeler.

'Culture is a source of exchange, innovation and creativity. It defines who we are and who we want to be. I believe indigenous cultures, knowledge systems and wisdom are vital to the future of humanity.'
Tom Wheeler

Indigenous people have had strong advocates walking beside them over time. Tom is one of these selfless individuals, and I am proud to call him a wonderful friend.

Above
With featured artist William Barton and other luminaries at G'Day USA.

Right
Sharing a life-changing moment with my oldest son, Nathan, at the National NAIDOC Awards in Brisbane is a moment I'll cherish forever.

Left

When Gary Green (middle) and Ben Hannesbury (left) invited me to create an exclusive series of art to adorn the Mount Yengo label, we collectively agreed the influence of culture and the beauty of land and spirit would truly represent our journey.

Below

Fellow Tasmanian Rodney Dillon's work as an activist is renowned across the globe. NAIDOC male Person of the Year in 2006 and winner of the 2013 Tasmanian Human Rights Award, he is an inspiration.

Above

Influenced by global culture, my creations transcend the ethnographic realm. Each installation takes on a life of its own, absorbing then reflecting the essence of the land the works live on.

This exhibition at the Citadel de San Francisco in Cuba, opened by Fidel 'Fidelito' Castro Diaz-Balart, was a unique blend of traditional photographs and my creative series of natural artworks from the 'Lowanna' series.

Skippy

Capturing the moment
with a camera is
second nature;
remembering the sound
of kids laughing and
yelling as they bounced
across the scorching
red dust in sugarbags
is unforgettable.
They called this game
Skippy. The photo was
taken in Hermannsburg,
Northern Territory, a
couple of hours west of
Alice Springs. As I was
sitting in the middle of
the oval with them all
bouncing towards me,
the joy of the littlies
having fun was so
infectious, I actually felt
like I was a kid again.

Above
At the Tiwi Grand Final.

Below
Imalu Tigers win the Tiwi Grand Final.

Opposite
'Culture, to me, means that I can draw strength from my people who have gone before me.

Our culture is strong and unbreakable, we are proud and resilient.

My culture has helped me to battle the tough times I've encountered throughout my life.

And now I must help others! It's everything, it's who we are!'
Michael O'Loughlin

Silently shifting to
the will of southern
winds, oceans of
sand ebb and flow
across the dark
silence, forever
destined to embrace
the spirits of
the ancestors.

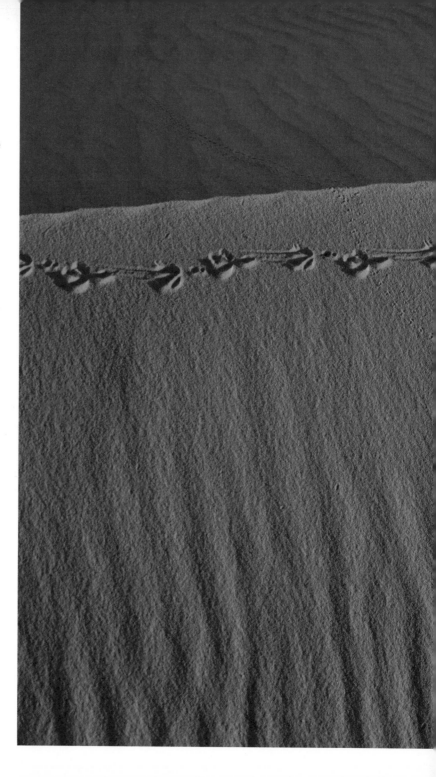

MUNGO MAN

Peoples of the Muthi Muthi, Ngiyampaa and Paakantji/Barkindji communities returned the remains of one of their ancestors to his traditional land.

Above
Djarindjin is home to the Bardi and Jawi people, 200 kilometres north of Broome in Western Australia. It is also home to the completely Indigenous-owned and -operated hot refuelling airport, which happens to be the largest in the Southern Hemisphere.

Opposite
Since the beginning, my work has explored connection with personal lived experience. Preconditioned ideas will judge this photo, but the story lies immersed in the truth.

The Wirrapunda Brothers

Humour is the best medicine, they say. I would have preferred a forty-four-gallon drum of calomine lotion over the laughter of the Wirrapunda men in this instance. After a feed of baru (crocodile), we were sitting back to watch another incredible sunset when I noticed a black cloud moving towards us. The family suggested I crawl into my swag and cover up. Within minutes the netting was suffocated by billions of mozzies.

It wasn't until the next morning that I discovered the tenacity and savagery of the little buggers. Red welts covered every inch of my skin, including the bottoms of my feet. The men couldn't stop laughing, saying that I had turned from blackfella to redfella overnight.

A few days later, the men said, 'Hey, Wayne, how about we get painted up, grab a couple of spears and head over to the airstrip and wait for this mob to land.' It was the federal election and each community is visited by two small aircraft – in one, the electoral officials, and in the second, the candidates and observers.

The look on the officials' faces when stepping onto the tarmac was priceless.

To listen to our old people, respect their connection with country and learn from their lived experiences is fundamental in keeping the stories alive.

Below
Stan Grant, Sammy Butcher and Troy Cassar-Daley.

Opposite below
Brooke Boney and Luke Carroll host the Supply Nation Conference in Sydney.

Above
'To me culture is everything! It is about my connections to family, and who I am in this world, it's about my country where I am now – and where I'm from and where I'm going. It's about my language, and even though I don't know it or speak it, I know it's still in me waiting to be released. It's about ... it's about my spirit, because it's what connects me to God, it's about laws that keep me on the right path. It's about love and respect for life and others that keep me strong to teach my children and grandchildren, and that's what gives me my identity – to be the proud Wollithican/Pangerang woman that I am. And when I create something, it comes from within, from all that is within me, my connections, my country, my language, my spirit, my culture.'
Neva Moirathaban-Wollithica Bangerang Atkinson (on right)

Above

'Culture is the sacred foundation of the health and wellbeing of our people. It is the identifiable past of tradition, connections to our creator, ancestors, songlines and dreaming. All things flow from our culture, creating balance – our traditions, values, knowledge, traditional food, medicines, spirituality, ceremonies, language ... everything. It is who we are and where we come from, our identity. As a Gamilaroi and Murawarri woman, I have a strong attachment to and respect for my culture, it's who I am.'
Jodie Choolburra

Below

'I am a Nhanda Yamaji man from Gutharraguda (Shark Bay) in Western Australia. I am a Garimarra Nuju (my skin name) and I follow my traditional cultural law and ceremony. As an Aboriginal man, this is my true identity, and it allows me to better understand my connection to my ngurra [country] and how to look after it.'
Darren Capewell 'Capes'

Above
Star-studded line-up at
the launch of the National
Indigenous Television Network
at Uluru.

Opposite
'To me culture is the foundation
of our Indigenous peoples – at
its core are our languages.
Culture is like the tree of life,
with every branch stretching
out to the past, the present
and the future. Culture is like a
family tree drawing us together,
connecting us all through
stories, art, dance and song.
The branches are many but the
tree is one – this is culture
to me.'
Christine Anu

Above
Dan Sultan

Opposite above
NITV crew chillin'
in the desert.

Opposite below
Christine Anu and
Casey Donovan
stylin' up.

This work is symbolic of how traditional knowledge and dreaming stories have merged artistic conjecture with a need to understand the concept of existence. Each artwork is a foundation to challenge the perception of truth by constructing realities from my subconscious. Do they represent a believable truth that questions the practicalities of a physical existence compared to one of enlightenment?

Above
Noodle races at the Woorabinda pool in Queensland.

Opposite above
The people of Tiwi are as enigmatic and colourful as the island paradise they call home. With the island only accessible by boat or plane, the children find unique ways of entertaining themselves, including playing with any animal they are able to catch, like this little piggy. I remember this so vividly, more for the squealing of the kids opposed to that of the pork bun on legs.

Opposite below
The acrobatics of kids in the bush never ceases to amaze.

Tjanpi weavers
The iconic Tjanpi Desert Weavers is a unique collective of more than 400 Aṉangu/Yarnangu women artists from the NPY (Ngaanyatjarra Pitjantjatjara Yankunytjatjara) Lands. Representing twenty-six remote communities scattered over 350,000 square kilometres of desert, the women earn an income from contemporary fibre art.

The kids of Mornington Island.

These photos were integral
to the success of the Closing
the Gap initiative, which was
important to all Australians.

Every morning the
school bus navigates
the streets of
Wurrumiyanga,
on Bathurst Island,
off the Northern
Territory coast.

Singing To The World
2003

Richard Frankland

If I were to look back at this life of mine

At times of folly, foolishness

At times of joy and conquest

At times of sadness, times of repenting

Times of great victories and times of smaller ones

Both of equal importance and equal meaning

At times when the world had crashed and the scars on my soul

Were unequalled in pain and sorrow

I would smile at my silliness

Be embarrassed at my joy, my ego, my loves and losses

Celebrate my victories and my times of losing

Rejoice in my recognition of the equality of a smile and the meaning of a gift and the beauty of a soul

I would shed tears at my times of sadness

And chase bittersweet memories across the dreamscape of the memories of my life

And finally I would lay exhausted with my heart laying rent open upon the hearth of my home

And I would sift through it searching for diamond drops of memories

And if one would see me in such a state

They would be prone to ask, 'What would you change?'

Nothing, not one thing, I would say

Then, after a contemplative moment

Except I would say whilst challenging myself

Whilst drawing a sword of courage and casting aside a shield of shame

I would shout loudly to the world, I would have sung louder

Smiled brighter

Given harder

Seen beauty quicker

Shared smiles more often

Hugged harder

Loved better

I would learn to play my soul better

I would paint teardrops so I could find happiness easier

I would have danced with more abandon and with more people

And also rejoiced in dancing alone

I would laugh at the small problems so I could help solve the big ones

I would see dreams in clouds and taste the future in morning dew

I would find thoughts profound in flames

And see the wondrous beauty in a small rock, a leaf, a single blade of grass, in a piece of bark upon a tree

From this I would know what makes a view majestic and a soul so small yet so big

I would worship the spirits of the untainted ones, the children, the meek, those unable to protect themselves

I would strive to heal the evils of the world and learn to love with an open hand

I would learn to write songs of humility and to plant seeds of hope and healing

Jack Manning Bancroft
and Bronwyn Bancroft

'The maintenance of
cultural frameworks
that benefit many
people because of the
longevity of knowledge
and how it is used in this
country is of paramount
importance to me as a
Bundjalung woman.'
Bronwyn Bancroft

'Culture ... it's alive.'
Jack Manning Bancroft

Above
Tiga Bayles was a true visionary, a man of substance, a warrior for his people and a long-time friend and mentor.

Below
Merrkiyawuy Ganambarr, Sienna Stubbs and Will Stubbs

Two tribes one voice at
the annual Dance Rites
gathering on the steps
of the Sydney Opera
House. Hundreds of
dancers from across
Australia come together
to share traditional
customs, language and
contemporary culture
with the world.

Archie Roach

Above
Watching as Yolŋu culture
continues on through
the young.

Opposite
The Mother of Native Title,
Ernestine Bonita Mabo

Above
'Culture is my essence, it is my
being and I am my culture.'
Damien Williams

'Breath is the start of my
journey, Story is the body of
my life and Legacy is what
I leave behind. Those three
combined are empty vessels
without CULTURE.'
Gman

'Culture is not only living proof
of our ancient existence,
it is also the celebration of
our survival.'
Mikaela KJ Simpson

Above
'Aboriginal achievement
is like the dark side of
the moon.

For it is there, but so little
is known.'
Ernie Dingo

Below
'Sixty-five thousand years of
campfires and bush tucker
and bush medicine and
the ancient songlines and
dreaming tracks and sacred
dances constitute a major
part of my DNA. Two hundred
years cannot eradicate that.
If you have not been able to
maintain your culture, then
you can sure as hell revive
it. Start with your name
and religion. Change your
English slave name back to
an original Australian name,
as I have done, and treat the
land, plants, animals, seas
and rivers and all people with
love and respect as we have
been created to do since time
immemorial. Since Walalu,
the great Rainbow Serpent,
first created us and blew life
into our moulded bodies.'
Murrandoo Bulanyi Yanner

'Culture is the story of my ancestors. It is the resilience of my parents, grandparents and my great-grandparents as our people went through the invasion, colonisation and into contemporary times, and passed on that strength and resilience. The world is ours.'
Nyunggai Warren Mundine

Above
Lola Forrester,
Caroline Briggs and
Sharon Forrester.

Below
Cathy Freeman
visiting the local
school at Galiwin'ku as
part of her activities
through the Cathy
Freeman Foundation.

PARNNGURR NGURRA

COTTON CREEK COMMUNITY

MARTU KAJAYAN NGURRA KUJUPAJANU - LUYAN YANGKULUYAN WURJALWU
WUPIJINGAKA

ALL VISITORS TO REPORT TO OFFICE

NGURRA PARNNGURRJU WARJARNU WILKAM

WELCOME TO OUR COMMUNITY

PULIJ NGAKULAMLAMPAJUKU NGA NGURRA - MILI WARNGKA LAJU - JUNU

PLEASE RESPECT OUR COMMUNITY RULES

NUU KANYJA NUU WAMA - KAMU NYINGKA NITURLJU WIKALJAPIRTI

NO DRUGS   NO GROG   NO SPEEDING

The small plane dipped and rose on the desert updrafts as it headed towards the small community of Parnngurr, about 370 kilometres east of Newman, Western Australia. When we arrived at the art centre uniquely designed to observe Martu jukurrpa (traditional law), the men and women sat divided, ensuring they could not see each other. After sharing a cup of tea and a biscuit, the old ladies took us out bush to a place where first contact with Europeans was made in 1964. We stood in the soak as the ladies shuffled to the spots where they had played as young girls. In language, they re-enacted the moment of seeing 'white ghosts' sitting atop four-legged devils and how they ran away so as not to be eaten.

Fabian Brown lives an extraordinary life. His reputation as a traditional abstract expressionist is lauded by many, but he continues to live in third world conditions. Inviting me in to his house that he shared with two other men, he asked me to use this photo to show the world how they don't have running water, electricity or any of the essential services most people rely on as a basic human right.

Proudly emulating his Uncles, brothers and cousins, this young warrior is integral to the continuance of culture.

Above
Aaron Pedersen

Opposite
My boots, my hat –
this young fella from
Borroloola.

Cultural interpretation is influenced by many factors, both tribal and individualistic.

Can we truly see culture through one 'lens'? And if so, how do we share a collective vision?

Above
Uncle Banjo
welcoming the crowd
to Tarerer Festival in
Warrnambool.

Opposite
Brisbane Broncos NRL
star Steven 'Pearl'
Renouf visits Barambah
Aboriginal Mission in
Queensland.

Left
Stockman, ringbarker, canecutter and politician, Neville Bonner grew up on the Richmond River before being sent to Palm Island Aboriginal Reserve. He became the first Aboriginal to enter federal parliament as a Liberal Party senator from 1971 to 1983.

This photo was taken at a small church in Brisbane in the early nineties, where he continued to fight for the rights of Aboriginal people. I still have the speech shown in the image.

Above

'Ngata, Wayne. That photo you took, wow! Thank you for sharing! I knew the photo existed but had never seen any from that night – this was the first in all these years. It really means a lot to me. My dad, Banjo Clarke, was sick with the flu and he asked me to attend so I could collect his trophy. I was sitting with Cuz Porky and family. After it finished, I jumped in my old 2-door Torana by myself and drove straight to the Fram Mish, to Dad's. Got there at 3 am. I went in to his room and switched on his bedside lamp and woke him up and gave him his trophy. Though he was unwell, it really made him happy to see that he was appreciated. I miss Dad dearly and that photo really means so much to me, thank you, great memories. xx'
Lee-Anne Clarke

Below

Miss NAIDOC – Indigenous women's role in the cultural, social and political arenas continues to evolve.

Dance Rites is Australia's national Indigenous dance competition, held on the steps of the Sydney Opera House. Traditional, contemporary, rural, remote and urban dance groups from across the country gather to ensure language, dance, skin markings and music is shared from one generation to the next.

Opposite above
'What culture means to me – for me, it grounds me in this business of all the hype; my culture, at the end of the day, brings me simplicity, walking barefoot on my country is a blessing and a privilege.'
Sean Choolburra